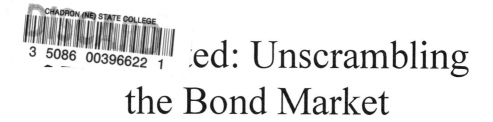

...ed: Unscrambling the Bond Market

RUSA Occasional Papers, Number 22

Sponsored by the
RUSA Business Reference and
Services Section (BRASS)

Lydia E. LaFaro
Editor

Reference and User Services Association
American Library Association
Chicago 1997

In September, 1996 RASD (Reference and Adult Services Division) members voted to change the name to RUSA (Reference and User Services Association). This RUSA Occasional Paper, Number 22 is a continuation of the RASD Occasional Paper series.

Published by the Reference and User Services Association
American Library Association
50 East Huron Street
Chicago, IL 60611

ISBN 0-8389-7921-1

Printed on 60-pound Starbright Opaque paper; bound in 10-point C1S plus UV coating by Batson Printing

The paper used in this publication meets the minimum requirements of American National Standard for Information Sciences-Permanence of Paper for Printed Library Materials. ANSI 239.4-1992

Printed in the United States of America

Contents

Acknowledgments

The conference program that produced the material for this publication was the work of the Business and Reference Services (BRASS) 1996 Program Planning Committee under the direction of BRASS Chair, Judy Nixon. Committee members included:

Lydia E. LaFaro (Chair), Arizona State University
Irwin D Faye, Chicago Public Library
Jacqueline Kilberg, McGraw-Hill Companies, Inc.
Mark Leggett, Indianapolis-Marion County Public Library
Tom Mirkovich, University of Nevada-Las Vegas
Robert W. Sears, Tulsa City-County Library System
Gary White, Pennsylvania State University
Craig Wilkins, Orlando Public Library

All members of the committee contributed to these efforts, especially Gary White, Tom Mirkovich and Craig Wilkins who compiled the glossary and the list of major bond indexes. Without their contributions and the supportive role of their respective institutions this publication would not have been possible.

Of course, a big portion of the credit must go to the program speakers Louise Klusek and Steven L. Lubetkin, who converted their oral presentations into a written format, and to their companies Salomon Brothers and Standard & Poor's Ratings Service, who allowed them to contribute their time and expertise.

Introduction

In early 1995, when the Business Reference and Services Section (BRASS) 1996 Program Planning Committee first met to choose a topic for the ALA Annual Conference in New York, we felt we had a unique opportunity to capitalize on the expertise of specialists located in the hub of the U.S. financial market. There are many aspects of finance that being in New York would have allowed us to explore. In the end, we chose bonds as our focus because it is an area so frequently overlooked that many librarians, especially non-business librarians, are uncomfortable helping patrons with questions on the subject.

The financial literature on bonds, itself, is not very helpful in this respect. It is either too technical or too focused on investment strategies for the do-it-yourself investor to offer the kind of concise, basic background knowledge needed by a librarian. In planning the program we wanted to offer an alternative approach geared to librarians that would provide a basic understanding of what a bond is, how to distinguish between different types of bonds, how to evaluate bonds and track their performance, and the most useful reference sources. Armed with this knowledge, librarians could feel more confident assisting patrons in identifying the correct information for their bond research needs.

We were fortunate to find two speakers with extensive experience in bonds who could offer unique perspectives owing to the different areas of the business in which they operate. The first was Louise Klusek who graduated from the University of Pittsburgh Graduate School of Library and Information Science and earned her MBA while working as the business librarian for the Graduate School of Business at Rutgers University. She worked in public, community college, college, and university libraries before going to Salomon Brothers in 1986. Salomon Brothers is one of the largest investment banks in the United States and has traditionally been known as the "Bond House." Ms. Klusek works as a research associate in the firm's Investment Banking Library which has a staff of sixteen, including five librarians, servicing the information needs of the Salomon Brothers New York City headquarters as well as the regional and worldwide branches.

The second was Steve Lubetkin, a veteran of more than eighteen years in corporate and financial communications and print and broadcast journalism, during which time he earned the designation "Accredited in Public Relations" (APR) from the Public Relations Society of America. He has a B.A. in Spanish and Philosophy from Monmouth College and an M.B.A. from the University of Phoenix. At Standard & Poor's, he has led the rating agency's expansion of credit quality seminar programs offered to bond issuers, investors, and financial intermediaries. In his position at Standard

Introduction

& Poor's Ratings Services he is both the director of their research library and the director of Global Ratings Development. He is an active Internet user and co-chair of Standard & Poor's World Wide Web task force, which is developing Standard & Poor's presence on the Internet. He has published articles on ratings, financial communications, and public relations in *Financial Communications Report*, *Standard & Poor's CreditWeek*, *PR Tactics*, *The Public Relations Strategist*, and SLA's *Business and Finance Division Bulletin*.

Their papers published here are drawn from the presentations they made at the ALA Annual Conference program for Business and Reference Services on July 8, 1996, including information taken from their overheads and from answers to audience questions. Supplemental materials that were distributed at the program or prepared since then have also been included as separate chapters.

We are pleased to have this opportunity to share the contents of our program with our library colleagues outside the confines of the Annual Conference and hope it is both useful and timely.

LYDIA E. LAFARO
Chair, BRASS 1996 Program Planning Committee

CHAPTER 1

Bonds and the Bond Market

Louise Klusek

What Is a Bond?

Bonds are debt instruments. Investors buying bonds are not buying a share in an entity but are loaning money to a borrower and therefore become creditors of that borrowing company or government. Bondholders receive a return on their investment in the form of regular interest payments, typically paid every six months, followed by a final payment at maturity. This feature of mandatory interest payments explains why bonds are often called "fixed income" instruments.

Bonds can be secured by physical assets or they can be issued based on the "good faith" of the company to service its debt. Bondholders as creditors of the company have first claim, before owners of common or preferred stock, in the event of bankruptcy.

Who Issues Bonds?

Corporations

Corporate bonds are issued by companies to finance expansion or to raise capital for other expenses. Bonds that are secured by specific assets of the company are recognized as senior debt. Debentures, on the other hand, are not secured by physical assets but are issued based on the good faith of the company to service the debt.

Federal Government

Unlike stock which is only sold by corporations, bonds are also sold by governments. The Federal government issues Treasury securities, and these bonds make up the largest sector of the bond market. Treasury bills, bonds and notes are defined by their maturity. Bills have a maturity of one year or less; notes mature in one to ten years, and bonds have more than ten years to maturity. Treasury issues are considered one of the safest investments because they are government guaranteed.

Federal Agencies

Treasuries are not the only bonds issued by the Federal Government. Agency bonds are issued by more than fifteen government agencies. Some of the largest government sponsored enterprises (GSE's) are familiar names: the Federal Home Loan Mortgage Association (Fannie Mae), the Federal Home Loan Mortgage Corporation (Freddie Mac), and the Student Loan Marketing Association (Sallie Mae). Other government sponsored enterprises include the Agency for International Development, the U.S. Maritime Administration, the Export-Import Bank, the Federal Farm Credit Bank and the Federal Home Loan Bank.

Municipal Governments and Agencies

Municipal bonds, or muni bonds, are sold by states or their political subdivisions, including counties, cities and public authorities. Some types of public authorities that commonly issue municipal bonds are utilities, educational institutions, housing authorities and transportation systems. There are two types of municipal bonds, general obligation bonds and revenue bonds. General obligation bonds are funded by property taxes, sales taxes, or income taxes. Because they are funded by taxes, they are generally subject to voter authorization in a bond referendum. Revenue bonds are used to finance specific projects and are funded with revenues generated by the project, user fees or a dedicated tax. A typical example of a revenue bond is one used to build a bridge or turnpike and paid for by the tolls collected. Revenue obligations are the preferred method of municipal finance today.

Foreign Governments and Corporations

Foreign issuers can also register and trade bonds in the United States. These bonds are called Yankee bonds. The Yankee market has typically consisted of bonds issued by the Canadian provinces, Canadian companies, European governments and large multinational companies. Foreign bonds are also sold in the United States through the private placement market as Rule 144A issues.

Common Bond Types

Floating Rate Bonds

Bonds are issued in a variety of forms to suit the special needs of the corporate issuer or the investor. Floating rate bonds allow the interest payments to change over the life of the bond. The rate is usually based on some financial benchmark such as the Treasury bill rate, or Libor, the London

Interbank offer rate. Floating rate bonds are called adjustable or variable-rate bonds if they are based on a longer term index that is set only annually. The dual-coupon bond is another type of floating rate issue where the interest rate is set for a certain number of years and then is reset at a higher or lower level.

Zero Coupon Bond

Zero coupon bonds pay no periodic interest but are sold at a large discount. The interest accrues over the life of the bond, and a lump sum is paid to the investor at maturity. Zeros are also called deep discount bonds because they are bought at a lower price than par value.

Convertible Bonds

Convertible bonds are bonds that can be exchanged for other securities, usually at a specified date and a specified price. Convertible bonds are offered as new issues or are part of a package offered to shareholders as the result of a corporate merger. Merger-related convertible bonds can be exchanged for cash or debt or the common stock of another company.

New hybrid securities developed in the last few years combine some of the qualities of bonds with those of equity. Often they are bonds that can be converted into equity or bonds that defer payment of interest. Some of the more common hybrids are LYONS (liquid yield option notes), MIPS (monthly income preferred securities), and PERCS (preferred equity redemption cumulative stock).

High-Yield Bonds

High-yield bonds, or what are also called speculative grade bonds, are those bonds rated below the investment grade of Baa by Moody's or BBB by Standard & Poor's. They offer a higher than average interest payment in return for the greater risk taken by the investor. In the past these bonds were commonly referred to as junk bonds because of their high default rates. Issuers of high-yield bonds are often young companies with a short financial history or companies that are in a restructuring or leveraged buyout situation. Another category of speculative grade bonds are the "fallen angels." These are companies that originally had an investment grade rating but have been downgraded because of a deteriorating financial situation.

Asset-Backed Bonds

Asset-backed bonds are bonds securitized by some financial asset. The largest number of asset-backed issues are backed by credit card receivables, automobile loans, and home equity loans. Some of the newer asset classes used to securitize bonds are aircraft leases, home improvement loans, and student loans. Recently bankers have speculated about using lottery winnings and death benefits as security for asset-backed issues.

For Further Reading

"America's Financial Markets—A Global Capital Pool." *Securities Industry Trends*, August 30, 1996, pp. 1-12.

Cantor, Richard and Frank Packer. "The Credit Rating Industry." *The Journal of Fixed Income*, December 1995, pp. 10-34.

Cotroneo, Jeanne K. "New Assets Enter Securitization Market." *Standard & Poor's CreditWeek*, October 16, 1996, pp. 19-22.

Ensor, Benjamin. "Taking the Lid Off Convertibles." *Global Investor*, March 1996, pp. 15-22.

"Guidance on the Road to Rating." *Corporate Finance*, July 1995, pp. 15-18.

"Hybrid Securities: Debt or Equity." *Moody's Global Credit Research*, August 1995.

Montgomery, Leland. "High Noon: Fitch Investors Service Takes on Moody's and S&P." *FW*, November 23,1993, pp. 58-60.

"Standard & Poor's Role in the Financial Markets." *CreditWeek International*, October 2, 1995, pp. 35-38.

University of Texas at Austin. LBJ School of Public Affairs. *A Debt Reference Guide*. 1995, http://www.window.state.tx.us/localinf/debtguide/.

CHAPTER 2

Bond Ratings

Steven L. Lubetkin, APR

How Did Ratings Start?

How did bond ratings get started? It was not actually ratings in the very beginning. It was an idea, it was a concept—"The investor's right to know." And the man who came up with it was Henry Varnum Poor. Henry, back in the 1860s, started compiling financial data on the railroads and canals in the United States, which at the time were the principal engines of the industrial revolution. There was no information, but there were lots of people who wanted to invest in them. Meanwhile, unscrupulous operators were literally printing stock and bond certificates overnight, creating fictitious railroads and fictitious canal companies into which investors were dumping their money. It is reminiscent of some of the speculative Internet stocks today. So Henry Varnum Poor came up with a way to get financial information together for investors. He started compiling it. The companies were not very happy with this information being disclosed. Many of them would not cooperate with him, but the investors found it to be a very useful tool and for a number of years Henry updated the *Directory of Railroads, Canals and Steamship Lines in the United States*. It has been reprinted and many libraries may even have one of the replica editions on their shelves.

The successor to Henry Poor's work was Poor's Publishing, which collaborated with John Moody on investment publications and index cards with investment information. These were sold on the street by runners to the various brokers. At some point, John Moody and Poor's Publishing went their separate ways. John Moody went out on his own and produced the *Moody's Investor's Manual*, which to this day continues to be a very important source of information. Poor's Publishing went on to compete with Moody's, began publishing bond ratings around 1920, and in 1941, it merged with the Standard Statistical Bureau to create today's Standard & Poor's. There have been many newer entrants into the rating business in recent years, such as the well known Fitch Investor Service. Fitch has become much more aggressive and has assumed a higher profile. Then there is also Duff and Phelps which continues to be very active in the ratings area. Meanwhile IBCA in the United Kingdom is starting to make inroads in the U.S. and other markets, although it is much more prominent in Europe. In Canada, there are two major bond rating services, Dominion and CBRS which is Canadian Bond Rating Service.

There are also rating services developing in some emerging markets. Countries are seeing the enormous liquidity in the U.S. capital markets, and they want to copy that in their own markets. They have concluded that having third parties make independent assessments of creditworthiness is a critical feature for their capital systems. It is a linchpin to achieving that kind of liquidity in their markets. So they are coming to the United States for technical assistance in designing a rating methodology for their markets. The big question for emerging markets is whether they are going to control rating agencies through the government or they are going to allow independent private companies to be set up with some regulatory oversight? It is one thing to have regulatory oversight; it is quite another thing to have the government actually dictating the ratings to the individual entities that are issuing bonds. Standard & Poor's has had technical assistance relationships with several rating agencies in these markets overseas. One of these relationships has been with a rating agency in India called CRISIL (Credit Rating and Information Services of India, Ltd.). In Thailand, it has been with the Thai Rating and Information Service (TRIS); and in Mexico, with a firm that Standard and Poor's acquired several years ago, Calificadora de Valores (CAVAL), the leading rating agency in Mexico.

What's an NRSRO?

It is important to remember that rating agencies in the U.S. are officially sanctioned as Nationally Recognized Statistical Rating Organizations or NRSRO's. This is a designation that is written into the securities laws in the United States. Back in the 1930s and 1940s, when the securities markets were coming under increasing regulation because of all of the abuses of the 20s and 30s, the securities regulators wrote into the law that securities issued in the U.S., debt securities, had to be rated by one of these NRSRO's. For many years, Standard & Poor's and Moody's were the primary organizations to which this applied. Now, as noted earlier, there are new ones that have come along in recent years. In the U.S., there are six rating agencies that are officially sanctioned by the government. These are Standard & Poor's, Moody's, Duff and Phelps, IBCA, Fitch and Thomson BankWatch. The last one is an NRSRO in the U.S. for banks. The other rating agencies are designated to rate anything.

What Do Rating Agencies Do?

What do rating agencies do? They offer an opinion. They analyze the creditworthiness of a company and give an opinion on the likelihood that it will pay its debt in a timely fashion. Except in the case of hybrid bonds, they are looking at two components. They are looking at principal and interest and they are looking at both of those things being paid on a timely basis. Sometimes the terms of the instrument itself can govern whether that payment is on a regular time schedule or whether it is tied to other market forces.

In recent years, investment banks have become very creative in designing bonds and bond-like instruments that look like they're going to pay in a certain way, but may not, depending on how things turn out in the market. This is particularly true if they are linked to an index. In some cases, there have been relationships to an index where if the interest rates rose three percent, then the value of the bond declined 20 percent because of the way the formula was written. So it is something that has become very complex and investors have to be very careful about it.

Ratings themselves are a shorthand expression that describe the credit risk. The "Rating Categories" section later in this chapter will describe the levels of risk associated with the different rating classifications that make up this system of shorthand expressions, but first it is interesting to note how amazingly pervasive the whole concept of ratings has become in general usage every day. It proves that people pay attention to ratings even though they may not fully understand them.

Take this example. A few years ago the Mets had a player by the name of Bobby Bonds. At one point, he fell out of favor with the Mets' management and the headline on the sports page in *The New York Daily News* was "Mets Downgrade Bond's Rating". It is mind-boggling how ratings have just become part of our everyday culture.

Here is another example. Last season there was an episode of "Law and Order"—it is a crime drama that takes place here in New York City—set on Wall Street. The police were investigating a case where the bond trader had been making some fake trades in bonds and he was suspected of murdering his boss. The police were interviewing a woman who worked with the suspect. They asked about her relationships with the men at her place of business and she said to the detectives, "There are only two types of men who work on Wall Street—standard and poor."

The Rating Process

Rating Request

The details of the rating process differ from agency to agency. At Standard & Poor's it usually starts with a bond issuer requesting a rating since the agency prefers to work with the cooperation of bond issuer in order to obtain the most information possible about their management, their strategies, their plans and their financial performance and condition overall.

Issuer Meeting

The next step is an issuer meeting where a team of analysts meets with the issuer's management. The analysts are experts in the particular sector that the issuer works in, whether it is a governmental, corporate, banking or other institutional type. They meet with the issuer's management, gather all of the information, and then when they have collected enough, they discuss it amongst themselves at what is called a rating committee meeting.

Rating Committee Meeting

The committee is composed of any number of Standard and Poor's analysts, including several senior analysts. The committee also includes people who have particular expertise. For example, when doing a rating on an insurance company, there have to be people who are expert not only in insurance company finances, but also people who know something about real estate finance because a big portion of insurance company investments tends to be in real estate. Or the committee might include analysts who have particular expertise in bonds of other institutions, because insurance companies also hold bonds from other issuers in their portfolios. So the committee process brings together experts in all areas relating to the issuer's business. It is very much a collaborative effort, though it does include an adversarial component when they reach the point at which the lead analyst who is presenting the credit has to defend his or her position to his or her peers as they play devil's advocate.

Notification and Appeal

Once the rating decision is made, Standard and Poor's notifies the bond issuer. The issuer does have the right to appeal the rating by providing additional information that may not have been considered or that the issuer feels did not receive adequate consideration during the rating committee process.

Dissemination

After the appeal is concluded, Standard and Poor's disseminates the rating through the news wire services. This is done through Standard and Poor's own internal wire service (CreditWire), which is not only sold to subscribers but is also used to feed the major wire services, in the interest of full disclosure, and those wire services in turn feed the other news organizations.

Surveillance

The rating process does not end here. There is still a very important and final step, conducting surveillance. This means staying on top of the financial performance of the issuer, to make sure that they continue to perform in accordance with what they have stated, and in accordance with Standard & Poor's expectations of how they will perform over the course of the bond's life.

Definition of a Rating

A rating is defined as a current assessment of the creditworthiness of an obligor with respect to a specific obligation. There are three main factors considered in determining a rating. The first is the likelihood of default, that is, the capacity and willingness of the obligor to pay the interest and repay the principal in accordance with the terms of the obligation. The other two are the nature and provisions of the obligation and the protection afforded the lender in bankruptcy.

Rating Categories

As stated earlier, there are a variety of rating categories as demonstrated in the figure below. The distinction between "investment grade" and "speculative grade" bonds arose because of regulatory requirements that limit the types of instruments in which banks and other financial institutions can invest. These are generally the instruments in the "AAA" to "BBB-minus" Standard & Poor's rating categories. Investment grade is simply a shorthand way of saying those are the instruments that qualify for investment by those institutions subject to the federal restrictions.

Speculative grade or high-yield or, as they are popularly known, "junk" bonds are anything below that. These are the companies that exhibit weaker, not necessarily bad, credit quality; although with those in the CCC and the D categories down at the lower right of Figure 1, the financial situation is very weak. These are companies that have higher than normal credit leverage. This may be an indication that they have more bonds outstanding than the BBB companies or that they are growing companies. It doesn't necessarily mean that they are bad companies, but it does mean that their financial performance is weaker.

CAPACITY TO PAY INTEREST & PRINCIPAL IS			
Investment-Grade		**Speculative-Grade**	
AAA	Strongest	BB+	
		BB	Least Speculative
AA+		BB-	
AA	Very Strong		
AA-		B+	
		B	Speculative
A+		B-	
A	Strong		
A-		CCC	Highly Speculative
		CC	
BBB+			
BBB	Adequate	C	Non-Paying Income Bonds
BBB-			
		D	In Default

FIGURE 1   Standard & Poor's Rating Categories

New Rating Services

The markets are expanding and there is growing demand for new rating services. For example, Chapter One elaborated a bit on the different types of bonds including asset-backed bonds, among which there are those based on lottery winnings. These are part of a new category of assets that are being used to securitize bonds. Even assets like health club memberships could be used as collateral for bonds. That has not happened yet but people are exploring it and the way it might work. Actually, it is not as strange as it sounds. It simply takes a pool of receivables and uses them as the cash flow collateral for the bond itself. In the case of lottery winnings, the cash flow collateral is a stream of future income. So it is not that strange, although some of the things that people have looked at securitizing sound strange at first.

Another one that has recently gotten a lot of attention is viatical settlements. These are insurance settlements for terminally ill people where the terminally ill patient wants to get access to the life insurance benefits before the time that those benefits would normally be paid. They may need the cash to pay medical expenses or to engage in activities that they want to pursue in the limited time they have left. There are companies that will pay terminally ill patients a present value cash settlement in return for becoming the beneficiary on their insurance policy. These firms will continue to pay the premium on the policy and the policies then go into a pool which is used to securitize bonds. It is actually a win-win situation. The advocates for many terminally ill patients, particularly AIDS patients, have really pushed this kind of issue where the insurance companies were unwilling to take the risk at first.

Asset-backed bonds based on auto loans and credit cards were also mentioned in Chapter One. If you wonder why you are getting so many solicitations for credit cards in the mail, it is because there is a financial machine that needs to be fed. It is the securitization of credit card receivables into bonds which is spurred on by the demand of investors who want the yields that these bonds will pay. The bonds have very high credit quality because, not only are they backed by the collateral of the credit card receivables themselves, but the banks know within decimal points how many of them are going to default. The percentage is really very small. Between four and five percent of credit cards actually default and do not pay. So they know how big a pool they need to have and they know how much additional cash they need to put into it. It is a very attractive proposition. Credit becomes freer and more available and both consumers and the credit companies are happy.

Counterparty Ratings

There are some other new types of services that Standard and Poor's is providing, such as counterparty ratings in the derivatives world. Derivatives or hybrids or whatever you want to call them are basically instruments that are based on other instruments. For instance, a stock option is a derivative because it is based on the price of the underlying stock it represents. The price of the option fluctuates depending on the price of the stock and how close you are to the expiration date of the option.

Derivative Product Companies

There are many other kinds of derivatives, too many to go into here. They have proliferated to such an extent that there are now companies set up as highly capitalized, high credit quality subsidiaries to handle them. They are called derivative product companies. They get ratings from Standard & Poor's and the other rating agencies as counterparties. The rating assures investors engaging in these various derivatives transactions—in essence, trading their interest streams for another entity's interest streams—that the counterparty they are trading with has very high credit quality and will honor the obligation when it comes time to actually transfer the money in both directions.

Corporate Credit Assessments

Standard & Poor's is also starting to do corporate credit assessments, referred to as corporate credit ratings. These are done for companies without publicly traded outstanding debt that are coming in for a credit rating from Standard & Poor's . They do this because they think the rating conveys important additional information they want their creditors to see, whether they are trying to negotiate a lease for a new office building or buy some equipment, and they need the bank to be comfortable with their credit rating.

Private Placement Ratings

Private placement ratings are a very active market. There are two basic types. One is true private placements where the debt is actually placed privately and there is never any public discussion of it. The company issues it; it is immediately sold to another company or a sophisticated institutional investor. Typically, an insurance company will buy these kinds of issues. But often, they want to have a rating on it because they need to make sure in their own auditing process that they are comfortable with the risk that they are taking.

There is another kind of private placement which is not as private and is called a Rule 144A transaction. It is named after the securities law provision that allows it to exist. Transactions of this type might be described as semi-private. They are made public in a limited way, but there are great restrictions on who they can be sold to in the secondary market, and most private investors do not deal in those kinds of transactions.

Project Finance

Project finance is a new, emerging area. In the emerging markets where there are infrastructure issues, there are roads that need to be built and bridges and airports and all kinds of pipelines and energy projects. The project developers are coming to the rating agencies for ratings on those kinds of issues. There are many factors that have to be taken into account, including the technology being used if it is an energy-generation project, the experience of the operator, and whether they have experience working with this type of technology. A lot of these are very risky projects. Standard and Poor's assesses the risk in a variety of ways, such as, looking at the contracts that an energy generator has with existing utilities to see if circumstances might make it a high-cost producer so that the utilities will not buy its electricity if the market turns against it.

"r" Subscript

All of these new issues have led to some new risks and that is what brought about the "r" subscript. Around 1994, Standard & Poor's started becoming concerned that the traditional ratings, the letter-grade ratings, were not adequately reflecting the risks that some of these instruments contained because many of the risks weren't just credit risks. There were a great number of issues, particularly from some of the government-supported enterprises, the Fannie Maes and the Ginnie Maes, where the notes themselves had components that caused them to fluctuate in value or fluctuate in the timeliness of the payments for reasons other than credit risk. If it is a Fannie Mae, it is going to be a AAA-rated instrument. But because of the way the note was structured, if the markets went up, the note might go down. Standard and Poor's became very concerned about this in view of the large quantity of them, so they created a subscript, a "rating highlighter", called the little "r." When it is appended to a rating, it is a flag to look for more information in the rating write-up in one of the publications or on the wires to see why we assigned that "r" subscript.

Bank Loan Ratings

Standard & Poor's is also doing bank loan ratings. Banks sell loans amongst themselves or trade them because they want to hold different pieces of their portfolio. The companies want to have some measure of credit quality, and Standard and Poor's has been working closely with the banking industry to come up with a methodology and a comfort level for them with the rating approach. The resulting ratings on the bank loans means they are traded more freely in the secondary market. It opens up transparency in the market; it opens up the liquidity.

Municipal Disclosure

This year the market saw an increased requirement for disclosure by state and local governments about the events that may have an impact on their credit quality. There were problems with the derivative investments in Orange County and in other municipal government portfolios and so one of the outgrowths of that is increased oversight, increased regulation. Municipal issuers are now required to disclose through a NRMSIR (Nationally Recognized Municipal Securities Information Repository), a very specific list of eleven kinds of events that are considered material events for municipal governments. They are required to make an announcement when those things happen, which can be anything from a change in their financial performance to the fact that someone was elected to the board or they have to change their name. So Standard & Poor's is now working with J. J. Kenny, one of its sister companies, on a service that looks at these events and determines whether it is important or not important, in the context of the overall credit quality. Some of these events are very routine disclosures that are simply required now, but there are others that have a serious impact and bear watching.

Claims-Paying Ability Ratings

Claims-paying ability ratings are the ratings assigned to insurance companies. These are ratings that assess the ability of the insurance company to pay its claims. It is important to distinguish between claims-paying ability and willingness to pay. The rating is only looking at the financial ability of the company to pay.

Conclusion

In conclusion, the demand for new ratings and new rating categories and new flavors is increasing. All of the bond agencies are aggressively competing; we are all trying to offer more and better services. The bottom line on ratings is that they are good for investors because they provide more transparency, more information on the market.

It goes back to the same idea that Henry Poor came up with 136 years ago when he said the investor has a right to know. With more complexity in the market for both the investor and the business librarian, the new ratings continue the tradition of providing unbiased assessments from which the public can make informed decisions. It is an exciting time of rapid change in the financial industry, calling for evermore specialized rating services.

CHAPTER 3

Sources of Bond Information

Louise Klusek

Introduction

This chapter provides a descriptive overview of the major sources of bond information. For a more complete listing of sources, refer to the bibliography on page 21.

Bond Issues

All publicly traded issues in the U.S. must be registered with the Securities and Exchange Commission (SEC) before they are offered to the public, and all investors in public issues must be issued a prospectus. The prospectus is the offering document that sets out the details of a new issue. The SEC's electronic filing system on the Web (http://www.sec.gov/edgarhp.htm) lists all public filings with only a twenty-four hour time lag. The Securities and Exchange Commission just last year also required municipal issuers to provide annual financial statements. The Municipal Reference Center (http://www.municipal.com/), sponsored by RR Donnelley, includes a Municipal Securities Disclosure Archive where all municipal offerings are listed by issuer and by state.

When a bond is brought to market it is given a unique identifying number, the CUSIP. Six digit numbers are assigned to each company, two more digits are added to identify the issue, and a ninth digit is added as a check digit. CUSIP numbers identify every actively traded security in the United States and Canada. CUSIP numbers are often used in databases and directories to identify bond issues. To find a CUSIP number for a bond, use *The CUSIP Directory*, published by Standard & Poor's for the CUSIP Service Bureau. *The CUSIP Directory* is published in an annual volume with weekly updates and in an on-line version.

Francis Emory Fitch, Inc. publishes guides, *Stocks and Bonds*, for the three major stock exchanges: the New York Stock Exchange, the American Stock Exchange, and NASDAQ. These directories list the CUSIP numbers of all traded stocks and bonds.

The *Moody's Manuals* provide descriptive information on particular bonds including call provisions, rights on default, the underlying security, and the purpose of the offering. Important identifying data for each bond consists of the issue date, the maturity date, and the names of the underwriters.

For Eurobond issues, the *ISMA Manual*, published by the International Securities Market Association, is the most comprehensive directory of issues. Bonds are listed by country and type: straight, floating rate, convertible, medium term notes and domestic bonds.

Bond Rating Agencies

Ratings

For the investor, ratings are one of the key ways to evaluate credit risk. Ratings provide a simple way to compare the investment quality of different bonds based on the likelihood of default or delayed payment. A high rating implies the issuer is less likely to default than an issuer with a lower rating.

Bond ratings are also used by regulators in the banking, securities and insurance industries. The National Association of Insurance Commissioners (NAIC) uses the ratings of securities in an insurance company portfolio to set capital requirements for that insurer. If an insurance company invests in speculative grade bonds, NAIC requires that they set aside adequate capital to cover the increased risk. The Securities and Exchange Commission also sets the net capital requirements for broker/dealers based on their credit rating.

U.S. Treasury issues are not rated but have an implied "triple A" rating because they are backed by the full faith and credit of the United States government and are therefore considered risk free. Most corporate and municipal bonds are rated. Some agency bonds are rated and recently rating agencies have begun to rate bond funds.

Ratings are given to both issuers and specific issues. Figure 1 on the next page compares the rating system used by Moody's and Standard & Poor's. Standard & Poor's further enhances its rating distinctions with plus and minus symbols. Both Fitch and Duff and Phelps use the same rating symbols as Standard & Poor's. Ratings for short term debt and commercial paper use different rating categories. The latest issues of *Moody's Bond Record* or Standard & Poor's *Bond Guide* contain a full explanation of the ratings categories. Also, the Standard & Poor's Web site (http://www.mcgraw-hill.com/financial-markets/ratings/) includes the full *Corporate Ratings Criteria* and *Public Finance Ratings Criteria*.

Moody's	S&P	Comments
Aaa	AAA	Best quality
Aa	AA	High grade
A	A	Upper medium grade
Baa	BBB	Medium grade
Ba	BB	Non-investment grade, some speculative elements
B	B	Speculative grade, high risk
Caa	CCC	In poor standing
Ca	CC	Extremely speculative
C	C	Moody's lowest rating
	D	S&P's default rating

Figure 1   Comparison of Moody's and S&P's Ratings Systems

Agencies

The Securities and Exchange Commission, which regulates the securities markets in the United States, recognizes certain rating agencies as Nationally Recognized Statistical Rating Organizations (NRSRO's). Ratings published by these agencies can be used as regulatory guidelines. Moody's Investors Service and Standard & Poor's Corporation are the largest and most well known of these services. Other NRSRO's are Duff and Phelps, Inc., Fitch Investors Service Inc., IBCA, and the Thomson BankWatch, Inc.

Both Duff and Phelps and Fitch Investors Service are well known second tier rating agencies. They rate all types of bonds but cover far fewer issues than Moody's or Standard & Poor's. Fitch has carved out a niche in rating mortgage and asset-backed issues. Recently they have added coverage of fixed income mutual funds. Duff and Phelps publishes bond rating research in four major areas: utilities, industrials, financial services, and emerging markets. They are noted for their research on public utilities.

Thomson BankWatch focuses on U.S. and international banking. Typically their bank analysis contains detailed commentary and statistics. They also publish reports on the banking environment in foreign countries.

IBCA publishes international bank ratings for over three hundred banks in twenty-five countries. Their ratings list is updated monthly and each bank is covered in an annual credit report.

Ratings Handbooks

All of the ratings agencies publish lists of their bond ratings. *Moody's Bond Record* covers over 68,000 issues. Publicly traded issues are indicated. Bonds are listed by type: U.S. corporate bonds, international bonds, structured finance issues, equipment trusts, commercial paper, medium term notes, deposit note programs, bank issues, counterparty, money market, insurance issues, preferred stock, U.S. government and Federal agency issues, industrial development bonds, pollution and environmental control bonds, and municipal bonds. For international issues, Moody's publishes a monthly guide called *Global Ratings*.

Moody's also compiles ratings in the *Annual Bond Record* which covers the entire year's corporate and municipal rating activity. Not only are new issues listed but there are lists of all issues maturing, all issues redeemed, and all issues with ratings upgrades or downgrades.

Standard & Poor's *Global Ratings Handbook* (formerly the *Ratings Handbook*) is the definitive list of Standard & Poor's rated issues with over 21,000 bonds listed. Corporate, structured finance, sovereign and international issues are included. The "Issues Section" gives the senior debt rating, the short-term rating, and the ratings outlook. Standard & Poor's also publishes a monthly guide to municipal ratings in the *Municipal Ratings Handbook*.

Fitch Ratings is the monthly guide to all Fitch ratings for corporate, municipal, preferred stock, and mortgage and asset-backed issues. Current rating announcements are also available through the Fitch Financial Wire and on the Fitch Web page (http://www.fitchinv.com/).

Ratings Analysis

Both Moody's and Standard & Poor's publish comprehensive guides to their ratings analysis. Standard & Poor's offers a *Credit Analysis Reference Disc (CARD)* on a monthly CD-Rom. This is their most complete rating service. It contains five years of press releases and bond analysis. A sample of the file can be previewed on the Standard & Poor's Web site (http://www.mcgraw-hill.com/financial-markets/).

Moody's publishes a *Corporate Credit Reports* series with in-depth analysis of issuers and topical reports on fixed income market trends and new products. The series is organized by industry sector and includes: Insurance, Industrials, Utilities, Banks and Bank Holding Companies, and Sovereigns. When Moody's issues a press release on a credit upgrade or downgrade, they appear as "Rating Review" inserts in the series.

Standard & Poor's publishes a unique industry-based approach to their ratings in the *Global Sector Review* which surveys the credit quality of industry sectors in five volumes covering industrials, utilities, transportation, and consumer products and services. The ratings rationale for all rated companies in each sector is included. Year-end ratios and statistics for all sectors are given in a separate volume, *Creditstats*.

Ratings News

Both Standard & Poor's and Moody's publish weekly news services that cover new issues and bond market activity. *Moody's Credit Perspectives* (formerly the *Bond Survey*) includes a "Bond Calendar" as well as summaries of many of Moody's special reports. New issues are featured with a description of the issuer and an in-depth description of the security with its terms, underlying security, guarantees, call provisions and more.

CreditWeek, the Standard & Poor's weekly, features major articles on trends in the industry along with selected company rating analysis. Since June 1996, *CreditWeek* has published with a global perspective replacing *CreditWeek International*. New or changed rating actions and a list of CreditWatch issues are included. A quarterly "Market Review" analyzes the bond market and includes a chronological list of new bond offerings. Selected features from *CreditWeek* such as the latest "Commentary of the Week" are also available on the Standard & Poor's Web site.

Standard & Poor's publishes *CreditWeek Municipal* for the municipal markets. Regular features include economic overviews of selected states and the S&P/DRI Regional Forecasts.

Credit Decisions, published by Duff and Phelps, provides weekly reviews of rated companies and a Ratings Watch list. Rated companies are given a full analysis with key fundamental data. Feature articles on bond market trends are included.

The weekly guide to all Fitch ratings is called *Fitch Insights*. Separate editions cover corporate and municipal issues. Each issue leads off with a viewpoint article and follows with issuer analysis.

Bond Alert Services

Because the quality of bonds can change over time due to changes in company finances or the bond market, investors need to follow the alert services for possible ratings changes. Securities that are under surveillance by Standard & Poor's are put on the CreditWatch list. An activity such as a merger, recapitalization, or regulatory action can prompt a CreditWatch listing. Standard & Poor's identifies potential credit implications for companies on the CreditWatch list as being positive, negative or developing. The company is removed from the list once the rating has been changed or maintained. The *Global Ratings Handbook* lists all issues on CreditWatch.

Moody's publishes their Watchlist for senior debt issues in the weekly *Credit Perspectives* and their complete list of Watchlist issues in the *Credit Report* series.

Wire services such as Bloomberg, Quotron and NewsEdge also distribute credit ratings news. All the ratings services provide press releases to the wire services. In addition, companies often release announcements of their ratings changes to the wire services or press release services such as *PR Newswire*.

Both Standard & Poor's and Moody's publish historical reviews of ratings changes. In Moody's *Credit Perspectives*, a quarterly supplement lists all upgrades and downgrades by issuer for both U.S. and international issues. Standard & Poor's publishes a "Ratings Roundup" each February in *CreditWeek*. It lists issuers, ratings changes, and the date of the change.

Bond Defaults

"Corporate Bond Defaults and Default Rates 1938-1995" is the latest annual report issued each January as part of Moody's *Corporate Credit Reports* series. All corporate bonds in default are listed and described. A useful chronology of each company's reorganization is included.

Standard & Poor's publishes a special report each May in *CreditWeek* which analyzes corporate default rates and rating patterns. Standard and Poor's also issues default studies on sovereign issues.

The Web site of the Public Securities Association (http://www.psa.com/) includes statistics and studies of municipal bond defaults.

Bond Texts

A classic text explaining the basic principles of the bond market is *Inside the Yield Book*, co-authored by Sidney Homer, one of the first bond portfolio managers on Wall Street, and Martin L. Leibowitz. The book covers the basics of how to compare bond values using coupon, maturity, price and yield. It also discusses how to match bond choice to investor preferences and includes a major section on bond portfolio management.

A comprehensive reference manual is *The Handbook of Fixed Income Securities* written by Frank J. Fabozzi and T. Dessa Fabozzi, now in its fourth edition. The Fabozzi's describe all types of fixed income securities and the latest valuation techniques. Basic non-technical guides are *How the Bond Market Works* and *How Municipal Bonds Work*, both written by Robert Zipf and part of a series published by the New York Institute of Finance.

Journals and Newsletters

There are several newsletters devoted to market conditions for bond professionals. For news of the municipal markets, the *Bond Buyer* is the newspaper of record. In addition to news of the market, it lists upcoming offerings and the Bond Buyer indexes. The *Bond Buyer* is published daily by the American Banker.

BondWeek is the newsletter of current events in the bond industry. This weekly covers the economy, market strategies, personnel changes and new issues. Regular departments include the "Bond Market Barometer" which measures bond indices, the "Financing Record" which lists new issues of the week, and the "Ratings Game" which lists ratings changes.

Investment Dealers Digest (IDD) covers the markets for stock and bond professionals. It often features stories on new financing techniques, unique new issues and profiles of investment banks.

For academic research on the bond markets, the *Journal of Fixed Income* offers in-depth articles by academics and bond professionals. It is published by Institutional Investor, Inc.

Comprehensive coverage of the Eurobond and international bond markets is available from the *IFR International Financing Review*. This weekly magazine covers the U.S. dollar market, bonds, loans, emerging market debt, equity and derivatives. Their focus is listing and describing new issues.

Associations

The principal trade association that represents the bond industry is the Public Securities Association. They are a major provider of statistics on municipal bonds, mortgage and asset-backed issues and Treasury and Federal agency securities. In 1995 they set up a corporate bond division. The PSA represents banks and securities houses that underwrite, trade, and sell debt issues. Their Web site (http://www.psa.com/) includes current issues of their newsletter, research reports, statistics and PSA standards.

The Securities Industry Association is the trade association for the securities industry with members from among broker/dealers, investment banks, mutual fund and money managers. They publish the *Securities Industry Factbook*, an annual guide to the U.S. capital markets, and two newsletters: *Securities Industry Trends* and *Foreign Activity*. Visit their Web page (http://www.sia.com/) for a full description of their publications.

The Government Finance Officers Association represents state and city finance officials. They issue reports and position papers on public finance management and audit issues. The *Government Finance Review* is their monthly journal.

CHAPTER 4

Bibliography of Bond Information Sources

Louise Klusek

Bond Issues

The CUSIP Directory by Standard & Poor's. Annual with weekly updates.
  Identifies CUSIP numbers assigned to every actively traded security in the United States and Canada.

EDGAR Filings from the Securities and Exchange Commission. Updated with 24-hour time delay.
  http://www.sec.gov/edgarhp.htm
  Electronic fulltext versions of public filings including the prospectus for any new security issues.

ISMA Manual by International Securities Market Association. Annual with supplements.
  Comprehensive directory of Eurobond Issues.

Moody's Manuals by Moody's Investors Service. Annual with supplements.
  Convenient source for bond descriptions for major corporate and government issuers.

Stocks and Bonds by Francis Emory Fitch, Inc. Quarterly.
  Series of guides for the three major U.S. stock exchanges listing the CUSIP numbers of all traded stocks and bonds.

Rating Agencies

Duff and Phelps Credit Rating Company
  55 East Monroe Street, Chicago, IL 60603
  312-368-3100

Fitch Investors Service, L.P.
One State Street Plaza, New York, NY 10004
800-75-FITCH
http://www.fitchinv.com/

IBCA Inc.
420 Lexington Avenue, New York, NY 10170
212-687-1507

Moody's Investor Service, Inc.
99 Church Street, New York, NY 10007
212-553-1653
http://www.moodys.com/

Standard & Poor's Corporation
25 Broadway, New York, NY 10004
212-208-8000
http://www.ratings.standardpoor.com/

Thomson BankWatch, Inc.
2 World Trade Center, New York, NY 10048
212-323-8300

Ratings Handbooks

Annual Bond Record by Moody's Investors Service. Annual.
Guide to the entire year's U.S. corporate and municipal ratings activity. Lists matured and redeemed issues.

Bond Guide by Standard & Poor's. Monthly.
Lists S&P ratings for many U.S. corporate issues of interest to private investors and selected munical bond issues and convertible securities.

Fitch Ratings by Fitch Investors Service. Monthly.
Lists all Fitch ratings.

Global Ratings by Moody's Investors Service. Monthly.
Lists Moody's ratings for international issues.

Moody's Bond Record by Moody's Investors Service. Monthly.
Lists of Moody's ratings for U.S. issues arranged by type.

Municipal Ratings Handbook by Standard & Poor's. Monthly.
    Complete guide to all S&P rated muni issues.

Rating Guide by Duff and Phelps Credit Rating. Monthly.
    All ratings, U.S. and international, plus "Ratings Watch."

S&P Global Ratings Handbook (formerly *Ratings Handbook*) by Standard & Poor's. Monthly.
    The definitive list of S&P rated issues. Covers short- and long-term debt ratings plus the outlook
    for all current issues.

Ratings Analysis

Corporate Credit Reports by Moody's Investors Service. Frequency varies.
    Series of in-depth reports organized by industry: insurance, industrials, utilities, banks and
    sovereigns.

Credit Analysis Reference Disc by Standard & Poor's. Monthly.
    CD-ROM system with both issuer and issue ratings. Also analysis and historical news releases.

Global Sector Review by Standard & Poor's. June to October in 5 volumes.
    Analysis of industry sectors with the outlook for all S&P rated issuers. Ratios and statistics in
    Creditstats.

Ratings News

Credit Decisions by Duff and Phelps Credit Rating. Weekly.
    Trends, news, and reviews of rated companies.

Credit Perspectives (formerly the *Bond Survey*) by Moody's Investors Service. Weekly.
    Summaries of new ratings plus economic news.

CreditWeek by Standard & Poor's. Weekly.
    New credit reviews for corporate and municipal issues. Feature articles. Now covers global
    markets that used to be published separately as *CreditWeek International*.

CreditWeek Municipal by Standard & Poor's. Weekly.
    Public finance ratings and industry trends. Features S&P/DRI regional forecasts.

Fitch Insights by Fitch Investors Service. Weekly.
All ratings actions, comments and FitchAlert for corporates and municipals. Available by fax or e-mail.

Statistical Sources

Bond Buyer Yearbook by The Bond Buyer. Annual.
Recaps the year in the bond markets with additional historical tables.

Chase Investment Performance Digest by Chase Global Data and Research. Annual.
Includes performance statistics for fixed income markets and indices.

Handbook of U.S. Government and Federal Agency Securities and Related Money Market Instruments by The First Boston Corporation. Irregular.
"The Pink Book" of government securities statistics.

Historical U.S. Treasury Yield Curves by Thomas Colemena, Lawrence Fisher and Robert Ibbotson. Ibbotson Associates, 1995.
Interest rate data covering 1925 to 1994.

Securities Industry Factbook by Securities Industry Association. Annual.
Data on U.S. Capital markets activity.

Bond Texts

Bond Markets, Analysis and Strategies by Frank J. Fabozzi. New York Institute of Finance, 1995.
Fabozzi's latest on bond analysis.

The Handbook of Fixed Income Securities by Frank Fabozzi and T. Dessa Fabozzi. Irwin, 4th ed., 1994.
Covers bonds, bond valuation and portfolio management.

The Handbook of Municipal Bonds and Public Finance by Robert Lamb, et al. New York Institute of Finance, 1996.
Covers all aspects of the muni markets for professionals.

How the Bond Market Works by Robert A. Zipf. New York Institute of Finance, 1996.
Basic guide to bond instruments and the bond markets.

How Municipal Bonds Work by Robert A. Zipf. New York Institute of Finance, 1995.
   All about municipal bonds, including bond math.

Inside the Yield Book by Sidney Homer and Martin L. Leibowitz. Prentice Hall and the New York Institute of Finance, 1972.
   The classic text on bond investment and the mathematics of portfolio management.

Journals and Newsletters

Bond Buyer by American Banker-Bond Buyer. Daily.
   Newspaper of the municipal bond markets.

BondWeek by Institutional Investor. Weekly.
   News for bond market professionals.

Euroweek by Euromoney. Weekly.
   Newsletter covering international capital markets.

Foreign Activity by the Securities Industry Association. Quarterly.
   Follows U.S. securities transaction activities by foreign investors.

Government Finance Review by the Government Finance Officers Association. Monthly.
   Journal covering public finance management and audit issues.

IDD-Investment Dealers' Digest by Investment Dealers' Digest. Quarterly.
   Features articles on new instruments and key players in the international fixed income markets.

IFR by IFR. Weekly.
   News on the global capital markets with a focus on details of new issues.

International Bond Investor by Euromoney. Quarterly.
   Features articles on new instruments and key players in the international fixed income markets.

Journal of Fixed Income by Institutional Investor. Quarterly.
   For academic research on the bond markets.

Securities Industry Trends by Securities Industry Association. Irregular.
   Features SIA statistics on the stock and bond markets.

Associations

Government Finance Officers Association
180 North Michigan Ave., Chicago, IL 60601
312-977-9700
http://www.financenet.gov/gfoa.htm

Public Securities Association
40 Broad Street, New York, NY 10004
212-809-7000
http://www.psa.com/

Securities Industry Association
120 Broadway, New York, NY 10271
212-608-1500
http://www.sia.com/

Additional Web Sites

The Blue List by Standard & Poor's
http://www.bluelist.com/
Search for corporate or municipal bond descriptions.

Bonds Online by 21st Century Municipals Inc.
http://www.bonds-online.com/
For the private investor. Look for brokers by state. Consult Moody's and Fitch ratings.

FDIC Library: Bank Rating & Analysis Services by the Federal Deposit Insurance Corporation
http://www.fdic.gov/fdicrate.html
The FDIC's guide to bank rating agencies.

The Municipal Resource Center by R. R. Connelly Financial
http://www.municipal.com/
Official statements, financial data, marketing materials, and links to state municipal agencies.

CHAPTER 5

List of Major Bond Indexes

compiled by: Gary White
                 Craig Wilkins

Bond indexes are statistical compilations of bond prices, yields, or ratios published in time series that usually provide comparisons expressed in contrast to a fixed reference or base year. A large number of indexes are compiled representing different types of bond markets. They are used as benchmarks in investment performance, as economic indicators, and in the trading of financial futures. Listed below are some of the major bond indexes.

Index Compiler/Publisher	Index Name	Source
Barron's	Best Grade Bonds	Barron's
	Intermediate Grade Bonds	Barron's
Bond Buyer	Municipal Bond Index	Bond Buyer
	11-Bond General Obligation Index	Bond Buyer
	20-Bond General Obligation Index	Bond Buyer
	25-Bond Revenue Index	Bond Buyer
	One-Year Note Index	Bond Buyer
Dow Jones	Twenty Bond Index	Barron's, WSJ[1]

Bibliography of Bond Information Sources

Index Compiler/Publisher	Index Name	Source
Dow Jones (continued)	Ten Utility Bond Average	Barron's, WSJ
	Ten industrial Bond Average	Barron's, WSJ
First Boston	Index of Lower Rated Bonds	Morningstar[2]
Lehman Brothers	National Long Bond Index	Morningstar
	National Intermediate Bond Index	Morningstar
	Municipal Long Bond Index	Morningstar, Bond Buyer
	Municipal Intermediate Bond Index	Morningstar
	Municipal Single State Index	Morningstar
	Auction Rate Preferred	Barron's
Moody's	Moody's Average Bond Yields by Type	Moody's Bond Record, Moody's Credit Survey
J. P. Morgan	Overseas Government Bond Index	Barron's
	Emerging Markets Index	Barron's
Standard & Poor's	Twenty Bond Index	Barron's, S&P[3]
	Municipal Bond Index	Barron's, S&P
	S&P Corp. and Govt. Bond Yield Index	S&P

[1]Wall Street Journal   [2]Morningstar Mutual Funds   [3]Standard & Poor's Bond Guide

CHAPTER 6

Glossary of Bond Terms

compiled by: Gary White (coordinator)
Tom Mirkovich
Craig Wilkins

Ability to Pay: The ability, present and future, for bond issuers to generate revenue in amounts adequate to pay principal and interest.

Accountant's Opinion: A statement issued and signed by an independent public accountant describing the examination of an organization's financial records. These statements serve to inform lenders of the borrower's condition at the time of examination.

Ad Valorem: Latin phrase meaning "according to value" which describes a method of assessing taxes on goods or property in which levies are based on an item's valuation rather than size.

After-Tax Real Rate of Return: The after-tax rate of return minus the inflation rate.

Annuity Bond: See Perpetual Bond.

Arbitrage: The simultaneous purchase and sale of the same or equal securities in such a way as to take advantage of price differences; buying something where it is less expensive and selling it where it is more expensive.

Baby Bond: A bond with a face value of less than $1,000.

Bank Discount Rate: The yield basis on which short-term, non-interest-bearing money market securities are quoted.

Basis Point: One one-hundredth of a percentage point. Example: A decline from 7.15% to 7.10% is a decline of five basis points.

Bearer Bond: A bond that does not have the owner's name registered on the books of the issuing corporation and is payable to the bearer.

Bid-Ask System: System used to place a market order. The bid price is what the dealer is willing to pay, while the ask price is the price at which the dealer will sell to individual investors. The difference between the bid and ask prices is the spread.

Blue List: A daily publication from Standard and Poor's listing bonds offered for sale with the price, yield, and other information.

Bond: A certificate representing creditorship in a corporation and issued by a corporation to raise capital. The company pays interest on a bond issue at specified dates and eventually redeems it at maturity, paying principal plus interest due.

Bond Anticipation Note: A short-term municipal debt instrument usually offered on a discount basis.

Bond Buyer: Daily newspaper published by American Banker which follows the municipal bond market. Included is an index often used as a yardstick against which bond yields are compared.

Bond Covenant: A legal agreement designed to mitigate potential conflicts of interest between bondholders and shareholders. Typically, covenants limit future dividends and restrict future debt. They may also address other areas of conflict such as claim dilution, underinvestment, and asset substitution.

Bond Equivalent Yield: A yield on a money market instrument or pass-through security computed so as to be comparable to a yield computed on a coupon security paying semiannual interest.

Bond Fund: A diversified portfolio of municipal securities sold to investors in units or shares by the investment company which owns the fund.

Bond Indenture: A document that defines the terms, or promises of a bond issuer, and guarantees certain rights to bondholders.

Bond Insurance: Insurance purchased by an issue for either an entire issue or specific maturities that provides for the payment of principal and/or interest.

Bond Issue: Bonds sold in one or more series authorized under the same indenture or resolution and having the same maturity date.

Bond Premium: The amount at which a bond or note is bought or sold above its par value without including accrued interest.

Bond Purchase Agreement: The contract between the issuer and underwriter that sets down the final terms, conditions, and prices by which the underwriter purchases an issue of municipal securities.

Bond Ratings: Evaluation of the creditworthiness of issuers and securities. Moody's Investors Services and Standard and Poor's are the largest rating agencies in the world.

Bondholder: Individual or institutional creditor who holds a contract by which the issuer agrees to make future payments in exchange for the advance of funds.

Bulldog Bond: A nickname for foreign bonds traded in the United Kingdom.

Call Feature: A provision in a bond indenture that allows the issuer the option of paying off an obligation, either partially or in full, before the instrument's date of maturity. The issuer is therefore able to retire expensive debt to take advantage of lower interest rates.

Call Price: The set price at which a bond may be redeemed by the issuer. The time period is established at issuance and the price is generally greater than par value to compensate the holder for the risk of early redemption.

Call Provision: See Call Feature.

Call Risk: The threat that a bond may be retired or paid off by the issuer. As interest rates drop, a bondholder may see the value of his/her investment drop toward the call price and, if the bond is called, he/she could be forced to reinvest the funds at a lower interest rate.

Callable Bond: A bond that the issuer has the right to redeem prior to maturity by paying some specific call price.

Cash Flow Yield: A yield on a pass-through security based on a projected stream of monthly principal and interest payments.

Collared Bond: A bond with a non-fixed, or floating, coupon rate that has an established minimum rate of return (floor) and an established maximum rate of return (cap).

Collateral Trust Bond: A bond issue that is protected by providing bondholders with a lien against an issuer's property, usually a portfolio of securities held in trust by a commercial bank.

Collateralized Mortgage Obligation: A type of mortgage-backed security in which the cash flow from a mortgage pool is distributed at varying rates of return, based on the bondholder's class or level of investment.

Commercial Paper: A short-term, negotiable certificate sold by one institution to another in order to meet immediate cash needs.

Glossary of Bond Terms

Convertible Bond: A bond containing a provision that permits conversion between the issuer's bonds and common stock at some fixed exchange ratio. See also: Exchangeable Bond.

Corporate Bond: A bond issued by corporations to meet financial obligations or to acquire assets.

Coupon: The annual interest payment made to a bondholder during the life of a bond. Coupon payments in the U.S. are typically made semi-annually, while Eurobonds pay once per year.

Coupon Rate: The specified interest rate payable to the bondholder. The coupon rate multiplied by the face value of the bond equals the coupon amount.

Credit Risk: The threat that the issuer, or borrower, will default on its obligation. Typically, the greater the credit risk, the higher the yield must be to attract investors.

Creditworthiness: The ability of an issuer to meet its obligations. Creditworthiness is rated by Moody's Investors Service, Standard and Poor's, and other credit agencies. See also: Bond Ratings.

Currency Denomination of Cash Flow: The currency in which the coupon payment or cash flow is paid. These payments need not be in the same currency used in the country where the bond was issued.

Current Yield: The ratio of the coupon rate on a bond to the dollar purchase price; expressed as a percentage.

Cushion Bond: High coupon bonds that sell at a moderate premium because they are callable at a price below that at which a comparable non-callable bond would sell.

Debenture Bond: A bond not secured by a specific pledge of property. Assets that are not pledged specifically to secure other debt may be used to satisfy any debenture bondholder's claims. See also: Unsecured Obligation Bond.

Debt Warrant: This allows the warrant holder to buy additional bonds from the issuer at the same price and yield as the bond with which the warrant was issued. See also: Warrant.

Deep-Discount Bond: Bonds selling at a large discount because their coupon is below going market rates.

Default: The failure of a corporation to pay principal and/or interest on outstanding bonds. See also: Credit Risk.

Discount Bond: A bond selling at a price below its redemption value.

Discount Rate: The rate of interest charged by the Fed to member banks in the Federal Reserve district.

Dollar Bond: A bond that is quoted and traded in dollars rather than in yield to maturity.

Doubling Option: Option that allows the issuer the right to retire twice the amount of debt required by a sinking fund. See also: Sinking Fund Requirement.

Dual-Currency Issue: A bond in which coupon interest is paid in one currency and the principal is paid in another. These issues are common in the Eurobond market.

Equipment Trust Certificate: A bond collateralized by the machinery and/or equipment of the issuing corporation.

Equity Warrant: This allows the warrant holder the option of buying the common stock of a company at a predetermined price. See also: Warrant.

Equivalent Bond Yield: A percentage used to express the comparison of the discount yield with the coupon yield of government obligations.

Essential Function Bond: A type of municipal bond in which the monies raised are used for traditional government activities.

Eurobond: A bond issued in Europe outside the confines of any national capital market. See also: External Bond Market.

Event Risk: External factors such as regulatory changes, natural disasters, corporate takeovers, or accidents that may affect a bond issuer's ability to meet its obligations.

Exchange or Currency Risk: When bond payments on a given issue occur in a foreign currency, domestic currency cash flows are dependent on the foreign currency exchange rate. The bondholder therefore incurs risk associated with fluctuations in capital markets.

Exchangeable Bond: A bond that can be exchanged for the common stock of a company other than the company issuing the bond. See also: Convertible Bond.

External Bond Market: The external bond market refers to bond trading activity wherein the bonds are underwritten by an international syndicate, are offered in several countries simultaneously, are issued outside any country's jurisdiction, and are not registered. The Eurobond market is a major external bond market. The external bond market combined with the internal bond market comprises the global bond market. Examples of an external bond are the "global bond," issued by the World Bank, and Eurodollar bonds. See also: Internal Bond Market.

Glossary of Bond Terms

Face Value: The redemption value of a bond or preferred stock appearing on the face of the certificate. Face value does not include interest, coupons, or other fees. See also: Par Value.

Federal Home Loan Mortgage Corporation (Freddie Mac): A private corporation authorized by Congress which sells participation certificates and collateralized mortgage obligations backed by pools of conventional mortgage loans.

Federal Housing Administration: A division of the Department of Housing and Urban Development, whose business includes insuring residential mortgage loans under a nationwide system.

Federal National Mortgage Association (Fannie Mae): A private corporation created by Congress to support the secondary mortgage market by buying and selling residential mortgages insured by FHA or guaranteed by VA. It also issues mortgage-backed securities backed by conventional mortgages. See also: Mortgage Backed Securities.

Flat Trade: A bond (or any security) that trades without accrued interest or at a price that includes accrued interest. The price quoted covers both principal and unpaid, accrued interest.

Floating Rate Issues: Bonds in which the coupon rate is reset periodically, based on the movements of a specified benchmark, such as the U.S. treasury-bill rate.

Flower Bond: A type of treasury bond selling at a discount that permits redemption at par value after the owner's death to pay federal estate taxes.

Foreign Bond: A bond issued by a nondomestic borrower in the domestic capital market.

Full-Coupon Bond: A bond whose coupon rate equals going market rates and consequently sells at or near par.

Full Faith and Credit Pledge: A phrase indicating that a government entity promises full taxing authority and other revenue streams to repayment of bond holders.

General Obligation Bond: A tax-exempt bond whose pledge is the issuer's good faith, credit, and full taxing power.

Gold Warrant: A warrant that allows the holder to buy gold from the issuer of the host bond. See also: Warrant.

Government National Mortgage Corporation (Ginnie Mae): A wholly owned government corporation operated by the Department of Housing and Urban Development. GNMA issues and guarantees mortgage-backed securities carrying no tax exemptions which are backed by the full faith and credit of the U.S. Government. See also: Mortgage-Backed Securities.

Guaranteed Bond: A bond issued by a subsidiary corporation and guaranteed as to principal and/or interest by the parent corporation. For example, government-owned companies may issue bonds that are guaranteed by their central government.

High-Yield Bond: Also called junk or non-investment grade bonds, these bonds have low ratings (below BBB) or are in default. They usually carry a higher degree of risk and a higher potential yield than other bonds, and are often associated with excessive leveraging, corporate takeovers, and leveraged buyouts.

Housing Authority Bond: A municipal bond whose payment of interest and/or principal is contingent upon the collection of rents and other fees from users of a housing facility built with the proceeds of the issuance of the bond.

Inactive Bond: A bond that trades only infrequently.

Industrial Development Bond: Industrial revenue bonds issued to improve the environment.

Industrial Revenue Bond: Municipal bonds issued for the purpose of constructing facilities for profit-making corporations.

Inflation Risk: The risk of the effect that real or anticipated inflation can have on the cash flow of a bond.

Interest Rate Risk: See Market Risk.

Internal Bond Market: The internal bond market refers to all bond trading activity in a given country and is comprised of both a domestic bond market and a foreign bond market. Also referred to as the "national bond market." The internal and external bond markets comprise the global bond market. See also: External Bond Market.

International Bond Market: See External Bond Market.

Inverse Floaters: See Reverse Floaters.

Investment Grade: A bond with a rating of AAA to BBB, as contrasted with a junk or non-investment grade bond. See also: Bond Ratings.

Junk Bond: See High-Yield Bond.

Letter Bond: Privately sold bonds that allow the investor to transfer or resell them.

Leveraged Buyout: Leverage expresses a firm's debt to net worth. Leveraged buyouts occur when a public corporation assumes considerable debt through the issuance of junk bonds in order to reorganize itself as a narrowly held company.

Long Bond: A bond with a long current maturity. A slang expression for 30-year U.S. Treasuries.

Macaulay Duration: An indicator that measures the price sensitivity, or volatility, of a bond to a change in yield.

Market Risk: Bonds sold before maturity may suffer a loss due to a rise in interest rates or other market conditions. Volatility is an expression of a bond's susceptibility to market risk. See also: Risk.

Matador Bond: A nickname for foreign bonds traded in Spain.

Maturity: Refers to the period of time in which the amount owed on a bond or obligation must be paid off. Typically, bond maturity is "short-term" (1-5 years), "intermediate-term" (5-12 years), or "long-term" (12-30 years or longer).

Maturity Date: Date at which a bond becomes due. Principal and any accrued interest due must be paid at this time.

Maturity Value: The amount an investor receives when a bond is redeemed at maturity.

Mortgage-Backed Securities: Bonds backed by pools of mortgage loans whereby investors receive the cash flow generated by the pool as determined by their investment.
See also: Federal National Mortgage Association; Government National Mortgage Corporation.

Mortgage Bond: A bond secured by a lien on property, equipment, or other real assets.

Municipal Bond: A bond issued by a state or local government or authorized agencies in which the interest paid is exempt from federal income taxes and is generally exempt from state and local taxes in the state of issuance.

National Bond Market: See Internal Bond Market.

Nominal Yield: Also known as coupon yield, the nominal yield is the annual interest rate payable on a bond and is specified in the indenture and printed on the face of the bond.

Non-Investment Grade Bond: See High-Yield Bond.

Note: An obligation that is due in less than ten years from the date of issue.

Official Statement: A legal opinion attesting to the legality of a municipal bond issue. This is similar to a prospectus in stock issues.

Offshore Bond Market: See External Bond Market.

Overlapping Debt: A bond having two issuers.

Par Value: Face value of a security. For bonds, it usually signifies the figure on which interest is based and the amount that is redeemed on maturity. See also: Face Value.

Pass-Through Security: A type of mortgage-backed security in which the cash flow from a mortgage pool is distributed to investors on a pro rata basis.

Perpetual Bond: A bond with no maturity date. Also called an annuity bond. Though they have infinite maturity, perpetual bonds are frequently callable by the borrowers. Perpetual bonds are common to the Eurobond market.

Premium: The amount by which the price paid for a security exceeds its face value.

Price to Call: The yield of a bond priced to the first call date rather than maturity.

Primary Market: Refers to the underwriting or auctioning of newly issued bonds. Non-central government bonds are underwritten by investment firms, banks, and other financial institutions, while central government bonds are usually distributed through an auction process. See also: Secondary Market.

Principal: See Face Value.

Prior Lien Bond: A bond that takes precedence over all other bonds because they hold a higher priority claim.

Private Placements: The act by underwriters of giving issued bonds directly to institutional investors rather than making them available to the general public.

Put Bond: A bond that can be redeemed on a date prior to the stated maturity date.

Put Provision: Allows the bondholder the option of selling the bond back to the issuer at par value on specified dates. See also: Put Bond.

Redemption: The retirement of a bond by the repayment of its face value.

Registered Bond: A bond whose owner's name is registered on the books of the issuing corporation.

Reinvestment Risk: The threat that future interest rates at which coupons can be reinvested will be lower than the yield to maturity at the time the bond is acquired. See also: Risk.

Rembrandt Bond: A nickname for foreign bonds traded in the Netherlands.

Repo or Repurchase Agreement: A transaction in which a party purchases a government security and resells it for the same price plus an interest charge.

Revenue Bond: A bond whose interest payments are generated from the revenue derived from operating the facility or project.

Reverse Floaters: Floating rate bonds that move in the opposite direction of interest rate benchmarks. Reverse floaters are typically used by investors as a hedging device.

Risk: A measure of the probability of an item not gaining in value. See also: Market Risk; Reinvestment Risk.

Samurai Bond: A nickname for foreign bonds traded in Japan.

Savings Bond: Bonds issued through the U.S. government at a discount.

Secondary Market: A bond market characterized by the lack of a centralized trading facility. Trading is usually conducted over-the-counter. In the secondary market, the liquidity of a bond is indicated by the spread between asking and bid price. The narrower the spread, the greater the bond's liquidity or marketability. See also: Primary Market.

Secured Obligation Bond: A bond whose payment of interest and principal is secured by physical assets.

Securitization: The act of acquiring loans and issuing a collateralized security that closely resembles a bond. This activity was pioneered in the mortgage-backed security market by the Federal National Mortgage Association and other quasi-official government agencies.

Serial Bond: A bond issue in which maturities are staggered over a number of years.

Series EE (Savings) Bond: U.S. government bonds issued in denominations of $50 to $10,000 at a discount.

Series HH (Current Income) Bond: Nontransferable U.S. government bonds that pay interest semiannually.

Short Bond: Bonds with a short current maturity.

Sinking Fund Requirement: A provision for repayment whereby the bond issuer retires a certain portion of an issue at regular intervals over the life of the bond.

Special Obligation Bond: A bond secured by a specific revenue source.

Split Rating: A bond having differing assessments as to creditworthiness from crediting agencies. See also: Bond Ratings.

Stripped Bond: The coupons on stripped bonds are separated from the body of the bond and both parts are sold separately. The body is traded as a discount bond and the coupons are separated by date and also traded as discount bonds.

Swap: A transaction in which a bondholder can exchange floating interest-rate bonds for fixed interest rate bonds, change the currency in which interest is paid, or change the benchmark base for floating interest-rate issues.

Taxable Equivalent Yield: The yield an investor would have to get on a U.S. government or taxable corporate bond to match the same after-tax yield on a municipal bond.

Term Bond: A bond issue in which all bonds mature at the same time.

Treasury Bond: A federal registered or bearer obligation issued in denominations of $500 to $1 million with maturities ranging from five to thirty-five years and having a fixed interest rate.

Triple Tax Exempt: A feature of municipal bonds in which the interest received is exempt from Federal, state, and local taxes.

Unsecured Obligation Bond: A bond whose repayment is backed solely by the creditworthiness of the security. Also called a debenture. See also: Debenture Bond.

Variable-Rate Bond: A bond without a fixed coupon interest rate.

Warrant: A warrant allows the bondholder the option of entering into other financial dealings with the bond issuer. See also: Equity Warrant, Debt Warrant, and Gold Warrant.

Watch List: A list of securities singled out for special observation by brokerage firms for potential credit risk, mergers, or other events.

Yankee Bond: Nickname for a dollar-denominated, foreign issued bond that is registered for sale in the U.S.

Yield: The flow of interest income generated by a bond.

Glossary of Bond Terms

Yield Curve: Graph depicting the relation of interest rates to time.

Yield to Call: The return available until the call date.

Yield to Maturity: The return available until the maturity date.

Zero Coupon Bond: A bond with no interest payments. Interest is paid at maturity. Zero coupon bonds are sold below maturity or principal value, appreciate as they approached maturity, and guarantee the holder a fixed rate of return.